This book belongs to

_____

WALT DISNEY® VOLUME 3
ADVENTURES IN
COLORS AND SHAPES

WALT DISNEY FUN-TO-LEARN LIBRARY

Adventures in Colors and Shapes. All rights reserved. Copyright © MCMLXXXIII The Walt Disney Company
This book may not be reproduced, in whole or in part, by mimeograph or any other means.
ISBN 0-9619525-4-7
Advance Publishers Inc., P.O. Box 2607, Winter Park, FL. 32790
Printed in the United States of America
0987654321

blue

The world is full of color, everywhere we look. Is there one color you like best of all?

Cinderella's favorite color is blue. Here she is in her blue dress, dancing with her handsome prince.

"I like blue, too," says the Blue Fairy. "When I wave my wand, I can make everything turn blue!"

Look! Pooh is painting the house blue—and Eeyore, too!

HUNNY

red

Winnie-the-Pooh sings a happy song as
he floats through the air:
"I like red la-la-la,
Overhead la-la-la,
And I hope you will note
I am wearing a coat
That's as red as red can be."

Captain Hook looks very surprised.
He's found a big red fish — and he
wasn't even trying!
What else is red in this picture?

It's the Fourth of July—time for good neighbors
to have a parade. Mickey Mouse is dressed as Uncle Sam.
Dewey carries the flag. Super-Goof is in the parade, too,
with Donald and Daisy, Minnie, and Morty and Ferdie,
Huey and Louie, and Pluto.

How many red costumes can you find? How many blue ones?
Which costumes are both red and blue?

yellow

Rabbit says yellow is his favorite color. Maybe that's because he is yellow himself. When he invites his friends for tea, he bakes a beautiful yellow cake and puts yellow frosting on it. Eeyore finds Pooh's present of yellow flowers quite delicious.

Alice finds a whole garden of yellow flowers in Wonderland. The yellow bread-and-butterflies come to say good morning. Alice thinks they are flowers that have learned to fly.

green

Robin Hood and his Merry Men are in the green forest — the place they like best of all. They have a big green sack full of money to give to poor people. It's so heavy, Friar Tuck can hardly lift it.

"Hurrah!" Peter Pan cheers, as the great green crocodile swims past him chasing wicked Captain Hook.

Minnie Mouse and Daisy Duck are very busy. They are having a super garage sale. Many of the things for sale today are green or yellow. How many green things do you see? How many yellow things?

MAGAZINES
25¢

gray

Little gray Dumbo is happy when he's flying over the circus parade. Here comes big gray Mrs. Jumbo, thump-thumping round the ring.

"Help!" shouts their clown friend. "I think I'd rather walk!"

What colors are the clown's suit?

orange

Look out! Here comes the great
orange tiger, Shere Khan. He's really
fierce, but Mowgli's not afraid.
Even the monkeys are laughing
at the big Shere Khan. How many orange
things can you find in the picture?

black and white

When Lucky Puppy and his brothers and sisters play together, there are white coats and black spots everywhere. Now they are having a tug-of-war. What color is the prize?

Flower the Skunk sees himself in a forest pond. "Oh my!" he says happily. "I never knew I was so handsome. No one else in the forest has a more beautiful coat than mine."

"Happy Halloween, everybody!" says Clarabelle Cow. She is dressed as a witch for her party. What color is her costume? Do you see something white? Mickey Mouse is the ghost.

Minnie is dressed as a ballet dancer in an orange tutu. How many other orange things do you see in the picture? What do you see that is gray?

pink and purple

Geppetto the woodcarver likes to make toys. Today he has made a toy castle, and he is painting it pink. Do you see another pink toy in the workshop?

Geppetto has made a toy elephant in a purple coat, and he has made other purple toys, too. How many do you see?

Can you see something in the picture that is black and white?

Bambi is very proud when he meets his handsome brown father in the forest. Who else, besides Bambi's father, is brown?

brown

The big brown ape-king is happiest when he's eating. Today his little brown monkey friends bring him fruit for his dinner.

What a wonderful time Snow White and the Seven
Dwarfs are having! Dopey has made bright new coats
for all of them. Have you ever seen such funny coats?
   Happy dances with Snow White. What color is his coat?
Grumpy wears a red coat while he plays the organ.
Dopey plays the drum. What color is his coat? Is there
a coat you like best of all?

circle

Timothy Mouse is happiest when he's at the circus. Today he's looking for circles there.

He finds an elephant riding a funny bicycle,

a clown holding a
hoop for his dog,

a balloon man selling red and green and
yellow balloons that are round,

and a seal balancing
something big and round
on his nose.

Huey, Dewey, and Louie are having a great time in their wonderful playroom. Everywhere they look, they see things that are square.

square

They see a toybox with square sides, filled to the top with toys, and a jack-in-the-box with square sides. It makes Louie jump.

Dewey uses blocks to build a big square wall. He checks to see if it is big enough.

Here is a picture of Uncle Scrooge as a baby. What shape is the picture?

"Who's afraid of the Big Bad Wolf?" sings the busy little pig as he hurries to cook supper for his two brothers. They are happy to be safe inside the brick house where the Wolf can't get them.

There are many round things in the picture. How many can you find? Now point to the square things you see.

triangle

Triangles are everywhere in Hiawatha's village. There is even a triangle at the end of Hiawatha's arrow. Something else is there, too.

"Go away!" Hiawatha shouts. "You are spoiling my aim!"

Sunflower is busy weaving a surprise for Hiawatha. It's a blanket covered with orange and yellow triangles. How many other triangles can you find in the picture?

For a special treat, Donald and Daisy took a balloon ride today. But look what happened! Now Daisy is wondering how she can rescue him.

There are many circles and many triangles in the picture. Can you find them?

Uncle Scrooge is happiest when he is showing his family how rich he is. There are many rectangles in his treasure room.

rectangle

These gold bars have rectangle-shaped sides. Huey and Louie use the bars to build a fort.

"Catch!" shouts Uncle Scrooge. He throws money into the air. Where are the rectangles in this picture?

This safe is shaped like a rectangle, too. It is full of jewels, and Uncle Scrooge lets Daisy wear them. Do you see other rectangles in the picture?

The Seven Dwarfs want Snow White to love their cottage as much as they do. Today they are building a path to the front door. They use stone that is shaped into rectangles, squares, and triangles. Which shapes do you see?

Look at the dwarfs' cottage. Do you see a big triangle? A rectangle? Look for some squares and some small rectangles, too.

Mickey Mouse is proud and happy when he leads the marching band. Can you find a big square and some small rectangles in this picture? Do you see circles and triangles in the marching band?

oval

diamond

"The world is full of different shapes," says Jiminy Cricket. "How many ovals and diamonds do you see?"

The oval reminds Snow White's stepmother of her magic mirror. Once upon a time it told her she was the fairest in the land.

Pooh's kite is the shape of a diamond. Hang on, Piglet! This diamond is going up into the sky.

heart

star

Clarabelle Cow says the heart is her favorite shape. She has baked a plate of special heart-shaped cookies for Valentine's Day.

"Make a wish!" says the Blue Fairy. When she waves her magic wand with the star-tip, the wish will come true.

"The best way to end a happy day is with fireworks," Mickey says. "I wish we could see fireworks every night of the year."

Mickey sees a square and a triangle. Minnie sees a circle and a rectangle. Do you see them, too? Morty and Ferdie know what color the shapes are. Do you?

Up in the sky is a whole rainbow of fireworks. How many colors can you name? Which color do you like best of all?